Table of Contents

Introduction

I want to thank you for downloading this book entitled, "Essential Cat Breeding".

This book was written for all cat lovers who are thinking about whether or not they should breed their kitties. The decision to breed any cat should always be considered carefully, planned meticulously, and prepared for with attention to the smallest details.

Today, there are a lot of stray cats that struggle to find shelter, enough food and clean water, all the while avoiding cruel owners or vehicular accidents. If you are reading this book, then you must be a responsible owner indeed! You are probably aware of how, too often, newbies in cat breeding make mistakes that often cost the life of the kittens and their mother. If you are looking for a quick, reliable and no-nonsense guide to breeding your cat, then you have found the right book!

In the following chapters you will learn all about some of the cat breeds that people all over the world have fallen in love with. Knowing the different kinds of cats will help you decide on which breed is right for you and your family, and how to match future kittens with good owners.

You will also learn about the basics of cat breeding. This includes how to tell when your cat is ready to mate, how to encourage mating, and the materials you will need to make your cat's pregnancy as comfortable as possible. Once you have mastered that phase of the breeding process, you will be ready to learn all about how to assist during the whelping phase. Breeders who know the correct techniques of whelping will be able to ease the birth of the new litter, and prevent any untoward incidents.

Lastly, there will also be a chapter discussing some training concepts you will be able to use with your new kittens. Trained kittens are more likely to grow up sociable and obedient. They will be easier to care for and rehome.

Are you excited to learn all about cat breeding? What are you waiting for?

Turn the page, and read on!

Thanks again for downloading this book, I hope you enjoy it!

Chapter 1 – Cat Breeds and Types

The first thing any cat breeder should know is the breed of their cat, as well as general characteristics and traits that apply to most felines. A basic understanding of the physical and behavioral traits of domestic cats will help breeders select potential mates for their pets.

Cats at a Glance

Domestic cats are scientifically named Felis catus. They are distant evolutionary cousins of the big cats, such as the tiger, jaguar and the lion.

A male cat is also called tom when it has not been neutered, while a female cat that has not been spayed is called a molly, though she may also be sometimes referred to as a queen.

Cats are lithe, flexible animals that are extremely light on their feet, and are capable of squeezing through tight or small spaces. They possess a high level of intelligence compared to other household pets like fishes and birds.

While cats are not as sociable and eager to please as their canine counterparts, they have nonetheless been part of the human household since the early Egyptians began domesticating them.

In general, cats have pointed ears, bright, big eyes, a whiskered short muzzle for scent identification and motion detection, as well as a tail for balance and speed. They have sharp teeth and retractable claws that aid them in their hunting and escaping ventures. Their senses of sight and hearing are superior compared to humans. They also have better night vision, and are capable of catching small prey like mice and birds.

Cats are known for their independent nature, and may oftentimes come off as anti-social. They are also territorial and keen on protecting their young ones. While caring for a cat need not be an expensive project, domestic felines nonetheless demand a lot of time and attention.

Popular Cat Breeds

Below are a few cat breeds that have consistently ranked high in the popular felines list.

1. THE PERSIAN

Long-haired and elegant-looking, the Persian has reigned over the cool cats' club since the late 1800s. They are known for their fierce loyalty and affection for their owners. Individuals interested in caring for and breeding this type of cat must remember that Persians need dedication when it comes to training and grooming. Their high intelligence demands engaging activities, and their long fur needs to be brushed every day in order to avoid tangles and mats.

2. THE MAINE COON

Where the Persian is known for its high-brow attitude, the Maine Coon is beloved for its warm nature, and loving disposition towards their families. The Maine Coon, second only to the Persian since 1992, has charmed both children and adults with their large frame, long fur and gentle gestures. Their fur is not as high-maintenance as the Persian, but families considering this breed should still prepare for its grooming needs, and basic veterinary expenses.

3. THE SIAMESE

Made famous as the villain of the cat world, the Siamese is a sleek, athletic cat that knows exactly how to communicate its wants and needs to its owners. These cats are among the loudest of the feline family. They often bond with one person only, but once they do, their loyalty and affection is unquestionable. Individuals interested in the Siamese cat must evaluate their lifestyle preferences, because this cat needs to be played with and occupied. Left home alone and bored, a Siamese can be destructive.

4. THE ABYSSINIAN

Abyssinians are not just beautiful to behold. They are also friendly and playful. They are often a great choice for households with children and young adults, as they offer excellent company. Thin and sleek, this cat is not as high-maintenance as the Persian or Maine Coon. They are excellent pets to have for those who are new to the cat world.

5. THE AMERICAN SHORTHAIR

These cats are famous for their hunting prowess. They were bred to chase and corner small prey, and are thus athletic and highly inquisitive. The American Shorthair is easy to train, and they are also great with small children.

Their fur does not need as much grooming as long-haired breeds, and they are generally more robust than other indoor cat breeds.

These are only a few of the most popular cats today. While they may have different physical traits, they do share their need for independence, loyalty to their families, and high level of trainability.

Remember that when you choose a potential mate for your cat, you must consider his or her breeding background, health and personality.

Chapter 2 – Breeding Your Cat

Now that you have a basic understanding about cat breeds and their traits, it is time to learn about the proper methods of cat breeding. First, you will have to ask yourself why you want to breed your cat. Below is a short checklist to help you evaluate your intentions, and decide on whether or not you should breed your cat.

Should you breed your cat?

Answer the following questions as honestly as possible. The results of this short quiz will help you determine whether or not you are ready to breed your cat.

1. Is your cat mature enough to be bred (at least two years old)?

2. Is your cat's vaccination and medication records updated?

3. Was your cat given a clean bill of health by the vet?

4. Is your cat's potential mate in the best health possible?

5. Is the potential mate's breeders knowledgeable when it comes to cat breeding?

6. Are you allowing your cat to mate in order to better the breed in general?

7. Will you be able to dedicate time, effort and money during the last leg of your cat's pregnancy, as well as the first few weeks after birth?

8. Have you done your research concerning your chosen breeds health characteristics and personality?

9. Is your cat's mate lineage traceable and of good quality?

10. Do you have enough funds in case of emergencies during the pregnancy and birth?

11. Are you willing to shoulder the costs of food, shelter, and vaccinations during the first two months of each and every kitten in the litter?

12. Have you thought about how many kittens you are willing to keep?

13. Have you contacted trusted friends and other breeders who will take care of the kittens you can't accommodate?

14. If a future owner suddenly can't provide for the kitten, are you willing to take it back and care for it?

If you answered yes to all of these questions, then you are ready to breed your cat. However, if you have even one "no", then perhaps you are not ready for the responsibilities of cat breeding. Please reconsider your decision to breed your cat.

Remember, if you are not willing to shoulder the costs and responsibilities of having a pregnant queen in your house, as well as a litter of kittens in the future, then you should not entertain the thought of mating your cat. Instead, you may want to spay or neuter your felinecompanion to avoid accidental pregnancies and other such incidents.

Kittens are a big responsibility. Their future should be planned for even before they are born. Think carefully about this stage of breeding your cat.

The Feline Estrous Cycle

Cats have a seasonal type of estrous cycle. This means that unless you breed them, they will have longer and more frequent heat periods. These periods of high hormonal urges often last from 14 to 21 days, but the estrous or the peak of the mating process usually lasts only four to seven days, depending on the age of the cat.

You will know that your queen is ready to breed when she shows behavioral and physical signs that she is in heat. The term in heat is used by cat fanciers to denote the period when queens are willing to be impregnated by a tom.

Below you will find the common signs that your queen might be in heat.

1. Your queen will have a swollen vulva.

2. She will be clingier, and may exhibit signs of separation anxiety.

3. She will be more affectionate towards her human family. She will often weave in-between the legs of her owners, or will insist on rubbing her face and muzzle on their skin.

4. She will often roll about on the floor, and may also shake her legs regularly.

5. She will twitch her tail and raise her hindquarters when you stroke her from the scruff of her neck towards the base of her tail.

6. Her cries at night will become more pronounced.

You can also ask your vet to analyze smear samples from your queen in order to be certain is she is truly in heat.

The Feline Mating Process

If you are reading this section, then it is safe to assume that you have evaluated your intentions and you are indeed, capable and willing to breed your cat.

Once you have chosen a suitable mate for your cat, you can place the breeding pair in an enclosed area and allow nature to take its course. You will have to ensure that the queen is ready to mate, and the tom is vigorous enough to assert himself with her.

The queen must be brought into the territory of the tom, since male cats mate better when they are in familiar surroundings. Once the cats have met, leave them in an enclosed area with a lot of space for them to move around in. If it is your queen's first time to breed, she may reject the tom's advances at first.

Allow the cats to get to know each other, and go about their business on their own. While it is not completely necessary for the queen to be in heat when she is mated, it will still encourage her to accept the male's advances.

It is best to breed a queen three or four times within 24 hours. After that, you must ensure that she is not allowed to roam, else she may conceive kittens from a different father. Be sure to record the date of the queen's mating in order to keep accurate track of her pregnancy.

Taking Care of a Pregnant Queen

The gestation period of a cat usually lasts 63 to 64 days, beginning from the day of conception. Sometimes, a queen won't give birth until the 67th day of her pregnancy. This is still considered normal, and is rarely a cause for worry.

Queens expecting a small litter will not begin to show an enlarged womb until the latter phase of their pregnancy, whereas queens expecting a large litter will have a heavy womb early on in their pregnancy.

Four weeks after mating, it is ideal that the queen be brought to a vet for examination. The vet will be able to confirm whether or not she is pregnant, and will also be able to assess her health.

As soon as your queen is confirmed to be pregnant, you must take extra care to prevent anything or anyone from bumping into her by accident. If a queen is jostled too much during the first few weeks of pregnancy, she may give birth to stillborn kittens.

Be sure that your queen always has enough food and water. You will have to increase her food intake as her pregnancy progresses in order to help her keep up with the nutritional demand of the growing kittens.

Consider feeding your queen only the highest quality of cat food you can acquire. You can also research the basic principles of the raw feeding diet in case you are looking for an alternate, more natural way to feed your cat.

Remember that your queen's diet will affect the health of her kittens as well.

You can also consult your vet regarding supplements and other such vitamins that will help ensure your queen has enough milk after she gives birth.

Invest in your queen's immune system. See to it that her immediate environment is always clean and free of fleas, and other parasites.

Make it a point to record any obvious changes in your queen's behavior and body, especially during the last leg of her pregnancy. Keeping a record of your queen's pregnancy details will help the vet in case of an emergency.

It is of importance that you have someone check on your queen every so often, whenever you cannot stay with her. Exercise her regularly in order to stave off obesity, and to help alleviate her stress.

Above all, exert as much effort as needed in order to make your queen's pregnancy an easy and pleasant experience. Prepare for whelping a week before her due date, and bring her to the vet at once if you notice anything strange with her body or behavior.

Chapter 3 – How to Assist in Whelping

In general, queens do not need that much assistance when they go into labor. However, as a responsible pet owner, you must make it a point to be there during the delivery. This way, in case something goes wrong, you will be able to help your cat, and possibly save her life as well as that of her kittens'.

In this chapter, you will learn about how to prepare for your queen's delivery, and how to assist her during the first few days after her labor.

Preparing the Whelping Box and Area

Be sure to prepare the whelping box and area for your queen at least a week before her expected delivery date. You can use a low wicker basket lined with old towels and newspapers as a whelping box. Of course, you can also build one from pieces of wood.

Make it wide enough so that the queen can move around during labor, and high enough that only she can leave the box when she needs to feed. Consider in advance how you will clean the box when the kittens are born.

The room where your queen will give birth must be disinfected and warmed. It must be free of drafts and cold wind. It is preferable if you place the whelping box in a secluded, quiet and dark corner of the room, in order to give your cat privacy. You can opt to place a heating pad under half of the whelping box in order to help keep the kittens warm.

Wrap the heating pad with one or two towels, and position it so that the kittens have enough space to move towards or away from the heat.

Signs to Watch Out for Before the Delivery

A lot of cats become extremely clingy to their owners when they are nearing their hour of delivery. This is especially true for first-time mothers. If you are not with her by the time she experiences her first contractions, she might try to delay her labor until you are with her.

This is why it is crucial to have a record of your cat's pregnancy. An accurate prediction of your queen's delivery date will help you prepare well and anticipate her needs.

In the last 24 hours before she gives birth, you may notice that your queen no longer has an interest in food. She will also become increasingly engrossed with the whelping box if you have already introduced it to her. Allow her to move the towels or layers of newspaper around to her liking.

You will know that her labor has begun when your queen becomes jumpy and agitated. She will not be able to sit for extended periods of time. Instead, she will walk around the room and pant heavily. Her stomach area will contract more the nearer she comes to giving birth. While she may not need you to comfort her, you must still stay near her, ready to assist her should she need you.

What to Expect When Your Cat Gives Birth

Once labor begins, you can expect your queen to deliver her first kitten within one to three hours. The kitten may come out head first or tail first. If the kitten comes out head first, then this is called a normal birth.

On the other hand, if the kitten is born tail first, then this is called a breech birth. Breech births occur about 40% of the time during whelping.

Within ten minutes, the kitten will be completely free of the birth canal. She will come out with a thin membrane wrapped around her face and body. This is called the placenta or afterbirth.

The queen should immediately lick the placenta from the kitten's face in order to stimulate breathing. If your queen does not go near the newborn kitten at once, you may have to intervene and remove the afterbirth yourself. You should also stimulate the kitten's breathing by rubbing her muzzle gently. You will know that a kitten has started to breathe once she begins mewling.

The queening phase should proceed smoothly after your cat has successfully delivered and cleaned the first kitten. The whole litter should be born within three hours. You can place your hand on the queen's midsection and press gently in order to feel whether or not there are other kittens waiting to be born.

If you observe that your queen has difficulty in giving birth to her kittens, or if she shows signs of pain and prolonged contractions without any delivery, then you may have to call your vet for assistance.

Sometimes, large litters must be delivered via caesarian section. Be alert, and have the presence of mind to administer first aid and support should your queen experience trouble during labor.

If everything goes according to plan, then your new litter will be contentedly suckling milk from their mother a few hours after they are born. All you have to do for the moment is make sure that they stay safe, warm and dry, and that they have all the milk they need in order to grow up healthy.

Chapter 4 – Basic Training Concepts for Cats

Like children, kittens learn fast. They need to adapt quickly to their surroundings, as well as the rules that their owners set down for them. However, training them can be a pain, especially since kittens often grow up into independent cats. This is why it is necessary to begin early, and to introduce a training method that will be easy for them to understand.

How Felines Learn

First, you will have to understand how your kittens are going to interpret everything around them. Since they cannot understand the human language, they will rely on your tone of voice and body gestures in order to puzzle out what you are saying. It will take some time for them to associate the word no with its various meanings such as stay away, drop that, or don't do that!

You can use the positive reinforcement method in order to make the training process easier for both you and your kittens.

This method of training is simple and easy to understand. To use it, all you have to do is make sure that you make every desired behavior pleasant for your kittens. For example, if one of your kittens urinates in the litterbox instead of on the floor, then you can reward her with a lot of treats and praise. This will tell her that she did something good, and that if she repeats this behavior, she will certainly be rewarded.

You can also opt to use the opposite training method: negative reinforcement. As the name suggests, negative reinforcement entails punishing a kitten whenever it is caught in the act of misbehaving. This means that you will have to make an undesired behavior's effect so unpleasant that your kitten won't want to repeat it at all.

This is, of course, less effective than positive reinforcement, because it also teaches the kitten that her owner is to be feared, and that her owner is capable of causing her pain. Choose your training method wisely, and stick with it to avoid confusion on the kittens' part.

Tips for Training Kittens

1. Start small and simple.

You should not expect your kittens to perform complex tricks within a matter of days. If you do, you will only end up frustrated, and your kittens will most certainly be stressed. Begin with simple commands. Make a list of house rules, and be sure that every member of the family understands how to reinforce those rules.

For example, you can start with the No climbing on the furniture rule, by consistently reprimanding the kittens when they try to climb on the couch, and by rewarding them when they play on the floor or when they get off the furniture as soon as they are told.

2. Practice, practice, practice!

Find time every day to train your kittens

to follow the basic house rules. You need not spend an entire hour bringing them back and forth to the litterbox, or using treats to get their attention. Ten to fifteen minute sessions daily will be more effective than forcing your kittens to sit through a grueling hour or more of listening to you lecture them.

3. Turn training into play time.

Make a game out of your training sessions as often as you can. This will

Essential Information for Breeding Cats

If you are considering breeding cats, there are several factors you need to consider before making a decision. It is not a job you should undertake lightly and we recommend reading up as much as you can on the cat breed you want to breed and what the process may entail.

Cat and kitten snuggling

In this article, we will provide you with a rough guide of what to expect if you do choose to breed. Consider seeking professional or expert advice though, and definitely try and speak to a certified breeder that you trust before making your decision.

Breeding cats and the law

When considering whether you would like to breed cats, the first thing you should keep in mind is the law. It is very important to check the laws on cat breeding and ensure that you can be in line with them.

The laws on cat breeding are not as strict as the laws on dog breeding. Dog breeding has two laws that regulate it: Breeding of Dogs Acts 1973 and 1991 and by the Breeding and Sale of Dogs (Welfare) Act 1999, which requires you to have a licence to breed dogs.

Breeding cats, on the other hand, is only protected by the Pet Animals Act 1951. This act requires you to have a licence to sell pets through a pet shop or an individual home; however, it is more than 50 years old and has failed to adapt to the changing cat breeding market, where most sales are made online and through small advertisements.

Recently, there has been a push from Cat Protection and MPs in the UK Government to try and rectify this. More attention is also being paid to the often poor conditions in which cats are being breed and it is likely that there will be strict crackdowns in the future. Cats Protection believes that much of these poor conditions are due to hobby breeders (those more interested in money than in breeding) so do make sure you are properly committed to the cause before breeding cats.

What does it entail?

Breeding cats can sometimes seem an exciting proposition, as certain cat breeds can sell for a lot of money. It is important to keep in mind, however, that the costs of cat breeding are high and that the process is time-consuming.

In 2013, the number of unwanted litters given to Cat Protection adoption centres across the UK increased by 19% from 2012. Most of these 'unwanted litters' were abandoned by hobby breeders who were not quite sure what they were getting into when they started and then could not sell their cats.

Here are some factors that you should keep in mind before deciding to breed cats.

Cat and kitten snuggling

Age of the queen: You should not starting breeding cats until your queen is fully-grown. If you do, it can be very damaging to her health, as she will then have to concentrate her energies on feeding her kittens rather than growing. Your cat should be 18 to 24 months old before you consider breeding her, and should be strong (i.e. healthy, and have a good body condition).

Health checks: It is definitely required for you to do a full health check-up of your cat before you consider using them for cat breeding. You should test for genetic disorders, any illnesses or diseases. They should definitely be free of ringworms and ear mites or fleas. You may also have to check with the vet on what breed-specific diseases they recommend screening for.

Breeding guidelines: While the official rules for breeding cats are not fully legally implemented, there are established bodies that play a crucial role in governing how cats are bred in the UK. One such organisation is the Governing Council of the Cat Fancy, which establishes breeding advisory councils that issue guidelines for each breed of cat. These guidelines include standard points, registration policy and breeding policy per breed. You may need to follow these guidelines, so make sure you are up to date.

Imported cats: There are specific rules for importing cats for breeding. Do make sure you are up to date with these rules and are following all the guidelines. The Governing Council of the Cat Fancy has some helpful rules on its website for what it requires to join its organisation and for registering imported cats.

Pet insurance: You will be expected to buy pet insurance for your litter of kittens if you are breeding cats. Make sure you have enough capital to cover these costs.

Vaccinations and care: You will also be expected to provide at least the initial vaccinations for the litter.

These are essential to making sure your kittens are in good health and that your customers are getting the healthiest cats possible. Vaccinations can cost a substantial amount when you consider that these kittens need to be taken care of as well in the first eight weeks, before you can give them to the new owners.

Seeking help

There are several unwanted cats in the UK and several more abandoned cats or strays, so do be sure you can find homes for your litter of kittens before you decide to start breeding cats.

If you are unsure and need additional help or guidance when it comes to making up your mind about breeding cats, there are several agencies that can advise you on the cost of cat breeding and what you need to consider. The Governing Council of the Cat Fancy is an excellent source of information on rules and regulations, as well as what you can expect. Their breeding policy and outcrossing policy should help you with any decisions you need to make. They also register bred cats in the UK.

International Cat Care is also an agency you can turn for advice on breeding. They provide information on international breeding standards and common problems to look out for.

In this article, we have outlined some of the factors you need to consider before breeding cats. Talking with an expert will give you more insight and help you make your decision.

What Does My New Cat Need?

Welcoming a new cat to the house can be an exciting experience. It can also feel slightly scary – maybe you even feel unprepared. Have you got everything you need? Will your cat be comfortable in your new house?

Cute tabby kitten sitting on cat tree

Do not worry – we have got you covered. In this article, we list the main things for cats you will need to have before you welcome them home.

– Crate

It is always important to begin with this essential piece of cat equipment. A crate is very useful for taking your cat to and from places – and chances are you will be bringing them back from the breeders' house or rescue centre in a crate!

A crate is essentially a space in which you can place your cat so that you can take them on journey. There are different kinds of crates: some are made out of fabric and others out of hard materials like plastic. These crates come with safety belts, to ensure your cat is safe on any journey you take her on. They can also be used as a safe space in the home.

Always choose a crate by asking: 'what does my cat need?' Remember to account for your cat's size, their strength and their behavioural habits.

– Bed

Choosing a cat bed is important, as your cat will likely spend a lot of time on it. There are several different kinds of cat beds available on the market, from beds suspended from windows, beds shaped like pods, beds shaped like chaise lounges and even beds shaped like castles.

Do not worry if you don't get the choice right the first time: picking the perfect bed may take getting to know your cat a bit and finding out what they love. Simply invest in a new bed if the old one is not a fit.

woman touching ginger cat on nose affectionately

– Litter box

Cats are mostly indoor animals and require a litter box for them to defecate in. This is one of the most crucial things for cats; you should take your time choosing what kind of filling you want in the litter box, what size works best for your house and your cat and where you want to position it in the house. Remember that the type of litter box you choose will determine how easy it is to clean.

– Food

Choosing the right kind of food for your cat is, of course, crucial. It is important to have this item on your checklist of new cat equipment before your cat comes home; you do not want the first mealtime to arrive and have nothing to serve them!

There are many types of cat food available. Try and choose a brand known for its nutritional value, such as a complete and balanced food from Purina. Different cats have different nutritional needs, so keeping your breed of cat in mind is very important.

Do not worry if your cat does not take to the food you have chosen; you can always change the brand under supervision from your vet.

– Scratching posts

Although it is not strictly necessary that you have this sitting at home before your cat arrives, don't underestimate how important a scratching post is on the checklist of important things for cats. Cats need to scratch: it is their way of keeping their claws trim. They also tend to rise up on their forelegs when scratching a post and thus exercise their whole body. Plus, if you do not bring this item home sooner or later, it is likely your cat will mistake your furniture for a scratching post instead!

There are several types of scratching posts available today. A simple one would be a pole covered in rough material that your cat can scratch. The more elaborate ones have levels on them for your cat to climb. Buy one depending on your needs and how much space there is in the house.

– Identification

Identification is an important answer to the question 'what do cats need?' Since outdoor cats are free roamers, it is likely they will stray from the house to explore the neighbourhood. If this happens, your cat should be identifiable by any stranger (so that they do not think your cat is a stray and try and adopt them!).

Most owners give their cats an identification collar with their details on it and a number you can call if the cat is found. Choosing the right size of collar matters, as you do not want it to be too tight around their necks but you also do not want it too loose, so that your cat gets a leg stuck in it when scratching. Most owners also provide their cats with a microchip; these chips can be scanned to reveal the same details as on an identification collar.

– Food and water bowls

Of course, you do not want to forget buying the equipment to put food and water in for your cat.

Choose a bowl that is the right size for the portions you need to feed your cat. You can also get more elaborate versions of a water bowl, such as a water fountain. A water fountain circulates the water in the bowl so that it is always aerated and fresh for your kitten throughout the day.

– Toys

No list of things for cats would be complete without adding. You do not have to buy too many toys, but make sure you have approximately three simple toys that you can rotate and use to play with your kitten or cat. Playing is a good way for your cat to develop their motor skills and cognitive abilities, as well as a good way to train them, so do not ignore this item on the list!

Hopefully you should now feel prepared to welcome your cat or kitten home. Simply make sure you have the items on this list and you are all set.

Conclusion

Thank you again for downloading this book! I hope this book was able to help you to learn all about the basics of how to care for and breed your cat.

The next step is to apply the lessons you have learned from this book to your cat breeding ventures.

Keep in mind that breeding a cat is a huge responsibility, and you should only do it if you are ready to support both the queen and her kittens. Of course, at the end of the day, as long as you love and can provide for your cats, you should be able to breed them without much fuss.

May your cats and future kittens grow up healthy and strong, and may you always stay in love with the feline queens of the house.

Printed in Great
Britain
by Amazon